Junior High Library
Brandywine Public Schools
Niles, Michigan

Bob Dylan

text **Kathleen Beal**
illustrations **John Keely**
design concept **Mark Landkamer**

published by **Creative Education
Mankato, Minnesota**

Junior High Library
Brandywine Public Schools
Niles, Michigan

Published by Creative Educational Society, Inc.,
123 South Broad Street, Mankato, Minnesota 56001
Copyright © 1975 by Creative Educational Society, Inc. International copyrights reserved in all countries.
No part of this book may be reproduced in any form without written permission from the publisher. Printed in the United States.
Distributed by Childrens Press, 1224 West Van Buren Street, Chicago, Illinois 60607
Library of Congress Number: 74-13936   ISBN: 0-87191-399-2

Library of Congress Cataloging in Publication Data
Beal, Kathleen.   Bob Dylan.
1. Dylan, Bob, 1941-   —Juvenile literature.
I. Keely, John, illus. II. Title.
ML3930.D97B4   784'.092'4 [B]   74-13936
ISBN 0-87191-399-2

Dylan Returns

"We want Dylan! We want Dylan!" For 30 minutes 18,500 fans waited in Chicago Stadium. Tense and expectant, they clapped in rhythm. They waited for Bob Dylan, the folk hero of the 60's whose songs and voice had influenced a whole generation. They waited to cheer him after an 8-year absence from concert tours. Finally the house lights dimmed. The audience was still. Then, as suddenly as he had left the American singing scene, Bob Dylan was back on stage.

The crowd went wild with applause. Without a word Dylan began his 1974 comeback tour of 21 cities. He would play 42 concerts to sellout audiences of more than a half a million people.

Then Dylan and The Band treated the fans to 27 folk, rock, country and pop songs that had brought fame to the young street singer of the early 60's.

For the first time in 8 years Dylan's fans heard him sing "Blowin' in the Wind," "The Times They Are A-Changin' " and "A Hard Rain's A-Gonna Fall." The fans loved this strong and simple protest music of the past decade.

Moving from protest to rock, Bob Dylan performed his electric, loud, banging songs. He sang "Like A Rollin' Stone," the most famous of his rock songs. Dylan then pulled the audience into toe-tapping country songs from his *Nashville Skyline* album.

Then on to a song from the *John Wesley Harding* album. Finally the superstar of protest music concluded the opening night of his concert by singing "Most Likely You Go Your Way (and I'll Go Mine)." He had to say once more that he couldn't stand still, couldn't be someone else's hero. He had to go his own way. Then as suddenly as Dylan had appeared on stage, he was gone.

In seconds, all 18,500 fans were on their feet, exploding in applause for Dylan. Flickering match flames lighted the darkened stadium. It was as though each fan wanted to say "Hello" and "Welcome back!" to Bob Dylan.

Standing in the wings, Bob smiled to himself. He had done it! He came back to sing after 8 silent years. He sang about past times. He pushed on to new thoughts, new songs. Dylan knew he had satisfied a hungry Dylan audience spreading across 3 generations.

Dylan's Magic

Dylan is a self-taught guitarist. He has always refused to take music lessons of any type. He plays a piercing harmonica. Some critics have compared Dylan's singing voice to a howling dog or a trapped bear. Dylan himself says his voice is ugly. What magic is it then that sent him skyrocketing to fame almost overnight in the 1960's?

Dylan's magic lies in what he says and how he says it. Most of his songs are stories, and most of his stories — even the ones that are hard to understand — are true. They tell people about themselves — all the funny and sad and hidden things people feel but can't put into words. Dylan magically finds the words. The magic of Bob Dylan goes on shocking and moving audiences all over the world.

Dream

Robert Allen Zimmerman (Dylan's real name) was born in cold and windy Duluth, Minnesota, on May 14, 1941. He moved with his parents and younger brother

to the nearby town of Hibbing when he was 6.

Bob's father managed a furniture and appliance store. The Zimmermans lived a very ordinary life, perhaps too ordinary for Bob. Later he would make up wild tales about running away from home and working in a carnival; but the truth is, he lived an ordinary life in Hibbing until he was 18.

In Hibbing the snow crusts the earth for almost 6 months of the year. The people of this mining town near the Canadian border are rugged and hardy. Although Bob often looks small and sickly on stage, he has inside him that same ruggedness that marks people of his north country.

From the time he was very young, Bob Zimmerman had giant dreams of becoming a rock star bigger than Elvis Presley. In junior high school he started his first group, The Golden Chords. Even then he was the *star*, playing guitar and singing wild songs in the style of rock and roll singer, Little Richard. Sometimes the audience enjoyed the act, but usually they booed him off the stage.

When Bob tired of one group, he would start another. By the time he graduated from Hibbing High, Bob had started and played with many rock and roll bands from Hibbing to Duluth.

On nights when he wasn't playing or rehearsing, Bob listened to an all-night radio station that played rhythm and blues. The way black people sang and played excited him, and he began to imitate them.

Bob is remembered in Hibbing as a loner. The only person he shared his dreams with was Echo Helstrom, his girl friend. Much later he would write a song about her, "Girl from the North Country." Echo knew that Bob had to leave Hibbing if he was ever to accomplish his dream.

In 1959 Bob enrolled at the University of Minnesota, only to flunk out several months later. He had skipped too many classes.

But Bob was not idle in Minneapolis. He took 2 major steps during his 15-month stay that affected his start in the music world. He changed his name to Bob Dylan; and he found a new and lasting hero, Woody Guthrie. Guthrie was America's greatest singer and composer of folk music.

It was clear to Bob, right from the beginning, that he had work to do in Minneapolis. He had to learn the skills of a professional singer, and he had to become known. It was also clear to him that having a long name like Zimmerman and wearing white buck shoes and buttondown shirts would not get him anywhere in the world of music at that time.

With his mind only on his music, Bob switched his college clothes for blue jeans and a ragtag jacket. He changed his name to Dylan and headed for the off-campus hangouts of Dinkytown.

Dinkytown was a colorful area of Minneapolis where artists and craftsmen gathered to sell their wares. Folk music was just becoming popular in the coffeehouses and bars of Dinkytown. Almost overnight Bob let go of his Little-Richard rock-and-roll style and began jamming with Dinkytown folk singers.

He liked the free and easy folk sound. Even better he liked the yarn-spinning stories of folk songs. He learned quickly all by ear, still refusing lessons in guitar or harmonica or voice.

With a harmonica strapped around his neck and a guitar on his knee, Dylan played at the coffeehouses and

bars whenever the owners would let him. Some nights he would make 2 dollars and a sandwich. Dinkytown audiences often booed Dylan. They laughed at his imitations of famous folk singers. But Bob kept on playing and singing. He had his dream, faith in his talent, and a rugged northern drive to keep going.

Bob had very few close friends during his stay in Minneapolis. Later those who had known him said that he was an unusual, charming person dedicated to music and to becoming a star. People were attracted to his innocent looks and sensitive personality. Bob often used friends. When he tired of one group of friends, he'd find another.

After he had become rich and famous, Bob began to realize that he had sometimes used people to help him get to the top in music. He tried to make it up to some of the friends who had helped him along the way.

Dylan had an almost magical way of being in the right place at the right time. Folk music was just coming back then. There was a need for new folk songs and singers. Bob was ready for the opportunity.

Then one day 20-year-old Dylan read a book that changed his life. The book was *Bound for Glory*, the autobiography of the great Woody Guthrie, who at that time was dying in a New Jersey hospital.

As he read the book, Bob followed the adventures of this writer of more than 1,000 songs. He read of how Guthrie travelled all over the country, singing out for the poor and deprived of America back in the 1930's and 1940's. Bob carried the book around for days, reading parts of it to his friends.

Dylan spent hours digging up Guthrie's old ballads, memorizing and imitating them. More than anything else

Bob wanted to meet Woody before he died and to sing him a song he'd composed just for him.

His friends laughed and teased Bob about his new hero. They were used to the stories Bob had made up about himself and his past. Some of his stories were about all the famous musicians he had met and the famous places he had been. So they laughed when Bob said he was going to see Woody Guthrie.

But Bob Dylan surprised them all. One day in December of 1960, he left for New York.

Giant Leap to Fame

"I froze right to the bone," Dylan once said, remembering the cold and damp welcome he received in New York City. Later he would sing about it in "Talking New York."

Bob went immediately to Greenwich Village, carrying his guitar and harmonica and wearing his famous corduroy Huck Finn cap. He asked the manager of The Wha? Coffeehouse if he could play there that night. The manager agreed to let him perform, but without pay. Quite unexpectedly for Bob, the audience liked him.

After a few days of playing and singing in the Village, Bob hitchhiked to New Jersey to visit Woody Guthrie. The experience thrilled Dylan. Best of all, Woody liked him.

Bob had composed his "Song to Woody" several months before meeting the famous artist. Shyly, Bob sang it for the composer who was now so paralyzed that he could barely speak. Woody was touched with the song and saw Bob as a real folk singer, not just a singer of folk songs.

Back in the Village, Bob continued to play the coffeehouses and bars. Sophisticated Village audiences could be heartless to a midwestern beginner like Dylan. They called him "hillbilly" and made fun of his Huck Finn cap and tattered jacket. Bob lived from hand to mouth, never knowing where he would sleep or work next.

But the struggle paid off for Dylan. He began showing up for Monday night hootenannies at Gerde's Folk City, a Village hangout. Soon the professional folk singers at Gerde's took notice of Bob's singing style. They noticed that he imitated the great folk artists like Woody Guthrie and Jesse Fuller. But they also noticed that he had the beginnings of a strong and creative style of his own.

Dylan began to "talk" a few songs at the Monday night hoots. They were all his own and some he made up as he went along. The songs were funny and playful, and the audience loved them.

Mike Porco, the owner of Gerde's, signed Bob for a 2-week show in March, just 3 months after his arrival in New York. Bob was excited and very nervous for the opening. Woody couldn't be there, but many of his famous friends were there at Gerde's to cheer Bob on. He wore an old jacket of Woody's. Dylan sang only 5 songs and was soon off stage — waiting. The applause was good. Finally, a break at last!

To be bigger than Elvis had been Dylan's dream. Suddenly the 20-year-old folk singer was well on his way to becoming the most exciting talent of the whole decade. In just one short year, Dylan signed a 7-year contract with Columbia Records and cut his first album, *Bob Dylan*. He performed in concert at Carnegie Chapter Hall. And Dylan became the first folk singer ever to be reviewed in the *New York Times*.

The album was unpolished and did not sell well at first. The concert at Carnegie Chapter Hall was poorly attended. Israel Young, who sponsored the concert, lost money on the affair. Still, both the album and the concert were starting points that few artists achieve in their first year of professional life. The biggest help to Dylan, though, was Robert Shelton's review in the *New York Times*.

Shelton had seen Dylan at Gerde's in the fall of 1961. His enthusiasm for the young folk artist came out in print the following day. Bob was very happy and excited about the review. He carried it with him for days and showed it to everyone.

Dylan's Music

For a time Bob Dylan was turning out protest songs as fast as he could write them and sing them. Joan Baez, the queen of folk music, liked Dylan's protest pieces. She remembers the first time she heard him sing and play his own music. She recalls being "knocked out" by the experience. "He really made me happy that there was somebody with that kind of talent," she said.

Once again, Dylan was in the right place at the right time. There was plenty of material for a protest songwriter with a talent the size of Dylan's: the war in Vietnam, the civil rights movement.

Young people in the 60's were angry. Nothing seemed to be done about the causes they cared about. Dylan's music seemed to bring it all together for them.

In "Blowin' in the Wind" Dylan asks simply how long it will be before every man will be treated as a human being. The song ends hopefully: "The answer, my friend, is blowin' in the wind." "The answer is coming," he says.

"The Times They Are A-Changin' " came out a year later and was much more daring than "Blowin' in the Wind." He tells people with closed minds to get out of the way if they can't understand why young people are angry with the false world around them.

As early as 1961, Dylan hired a very strong and aggressive agent, Albert Grossman. Dylan knew his job as songwriter and singer, but he needed someone like Grossman to handle the business part of his career.

Grossman was the right man for the job. He also managed the folk trio—Peter, Paul and Mary. When Dylan began producing protest songs, Grossman encouraged the trio to sing the songs and introduce them as Dylan's work. Dylan's name was soon known across the country.

By the summer of 1963, Dylan was famous in the United States and Europe. His greatest moment of triumph was the '63 Newport Festival, an annual event that draws artists and fans from coast to coast.

Present at the festival were Dylan, now king of folk music, and Joan Baez, the queen. The festival closed with all musicians on stage swaying, holding hands, singing in harmony the song that brought together the whole youth movement: "Blowin' in the Wind."

Newport left Dylan giddy with excitement. But already he was tiring of protest songs. Once again he denied being a leader of the movement. "I can't be responsible for those kids' lives," he told Joan Baez after the concert.

With the release in 1964 of his fourth album, *Another Side of Bob Dylan*, he began pushing on to new sounds and new songs. In "It Ain't Me, Babe," he tells people to look elsewhere for someone to fill their dreams. No longer protesting events larger than himself, Dylan began

to write about his own inner feelings.

Some Dylan fans were angry. Dylan had voiced their feelings and their discontent. Now, they thought, he was just playing music and getting rich. His fifth album was an even greater blow to such fans. In *Bringing It All Back Home*, Dylan changed from an acoustic to an electric guitar and added background music.

The Hawks, a polished rock group, teamed up with Dylan on that album. The group eventually changed its name to The Band. While they produce records and give concerts by themselves, The Band is best known for their backup music for Dylan. Together they create a sound that is unique and as varied as Dylan himself.

Dylan enjoys his background people as fine musicians and good friends. Because Dylan dislikes crowds and publicity, he and The Band spend all their time together when they're on the road. They jam, rehearse, play cards and have fun together.

As the title suggests, *Bringing It All Back Home* is Dylan's trip backward to his own roots as a teen-ager. The album sold more than a million copies.

Of all the songs Dylan has written, his own favorite is the rock song from the *Highway 61 Revisited* album, "Like A Rollin' Stone." In this song Dylan attacks people who live off the strength of others. In a slow, dizzy pace he snaps at the listener to get used to being on his own because that's the way it has to be.

Dylan fans were changing and had grown accustomed to rapid changes in Dylan. They were accustomed to surprises from him. But when Dylan sang "Like a Rollin' Stone" for the first time at the 1965 Newport Festival, the audience hated it. They booed Dylan until he fled from the stage with tears in his eyes. The hardened star,

who claimed not to care what his fans thought of him, really did care deep inside. Nevertheless, "Like A Rollin' Stone" rose to the top of the charts in 2 months and became Dylan's first popular hit.

After a whirlwind tour of the United States, England and Australia, Dylan felt tired and depressed. He went home to Woodstock, New York, to rest.

Motorcycling near his home on July 30, 1966, Dylan was thrown from his bike and hit the pavement hard. Recovery was slow, painful, and, like Dylan, very private. He seemed happy to be away from the concert-tour rush for a time.

As he grew stronger, Dylan began writing again and singing on records. Country music had interested him as a teen-ager. Now he explored it seriously.

Most country music is produced in Nashville, Tennessee, where music is a big industry. Dylan made a few trips to Nashville after his accident and was instantly turned on to the Nashville style.

Dylan's country music is gentle. *Nashville Skyline* came out in 1969 with Bob Dylan pictured on the cover as a country gentleman. The very tender song, "Lay, Lady, Lay," is the biggest single on the album.

The words of most of the *Nashville Skyline* songs

are light-hearted and clear as country fiddles and warm summer skies. It is music for the fun and joy of it, a new mood for Dylan.

Almost without noticing it, Bob Dylan had influenced rock and folk. He had taken folk music out of history and put it into people's lives. He had also put real poetry into rock music.

Never a disciplined writer, Dylan scratches out songs as they come to him. He says that the lyrics come first and then the melody. Often he'll borrow and adapt old tunes to his words. The words are more important than the melody to Dylan, but he does take care to put it all together skillfully.

When Dylan was working for Columbia Records, he had to write many songs to fulfill his contract. Otherwise, he once admitted to a reporter, he probably wouldn't have written so many songs. He said he would have been content just singing whatever he knew. Yet during 1962 and 1974, Dylan turned out 15 albums and many single releases.

Dylan the Prophet

A prophet is no different from other people, except for his vision. He sees things differently, more clearly perhaps. A prophet is not an action man. He is a seer.

Dylan is that kind of person. He never wanted to be a prophet, and he will continue to say he is not one. In "Restless Farewell," Dylan indicated that he is tired of being the Pied Piper. His songs have no meaning for the masses of people, he says. "It's for myself and my friends my stories are sung."

At the same time Dylan was never satisfied writing

the kind of empty songs that were often played on juke boxes when he started his career.

In his music Dylan looks at napalm bombings, senseless racist murders, hunger, hatred, dozens of dead oceans and poisoned rivers. In one song he looks at it all and says strongly that unless something is done about such a mad world, "A Hard Rain's A-Gonna Fall."

As a prophet, Dylan is not a square or a saint. He is remembered by many friends as taking a long time to grow up. Even with his ability to see the world more clearly than most people, Dylan was often selfish and confused.

For a time Dylan experimented with drugs and thought it helped his songwriting. Early in his career, Bob smoked constantly and ate very poorly. Now he eats a simple diet and has quit smoking. Dylan is proud of the smoother voice which replaced the sandpaper-rough voice of the early albums. "When I stopped smoking, my voice changed drastically. I couldn't believe it myself," Dylan told an interviewer.

A gentler prophet now, Dylan no longer scolds audiences as regularly as he did in his early songs. He tells them they don't need a weatherman to know which way the wind is blowing. They don't need him to save their lives.

Dylan goes on refusing to be anyone's prophet except his own. Yet he continues to write songs that make people think about their lives and the world around them. He seems to understand himself and his audience as he grows older.

Dylan is a very private person. Interviews and public appearances are painful events for the shy and sensitive Dylan.

Like the Beatles and many rock superstars, Dylan has been mobbed and mauled by screaming teen-agers after a performance. Having had parts of his clothing torn off and, in one case, a lock of his hair cut from his head, Bob Dylan is very much frightened by crowds.

Occasionally he will send a Dylan-double out the stage door and then later escape quietly through another door. Once he hid for 2 hours in the closet of his dressing room, afraid to face the mob. Another time he fainted when the crowd crushed in upon him.

Dylan once told friends, "Wish I could do it all and stay in the places I'm comfortable — where they don't stare at me. The attention is too much commotion for my body and head. The world's scary sometimes."

Yet Dylan knows he is both a public figure and a private person. He knows that if he wants his music to be known, he must submit to interviews from time to time.

What little publicity Dylan seeks, he uses well. Fans hang onto every word about him that appears in print. They hope to find out what he's really saying in his songs and what his private life is all about.

Now that he is older and interested in his comeback, Dylan is more patient with reporters than he once was. Since his nearly fatal motorcycle crash, his interviews reveal a side of Dylan rarely seen in his songs. Dylan is a very humorous man. When a reporter asks a silly question, Dylan responds with an even sillier answer.

Dylan believes strongly that no one has a right to information about him or his family. Strangely enough, most Dylan fans agree to his need for privacy. They satisfy themselves with crumbs of information about Dylan, the private man.

Very little is known about Sarah Lowndes who mar-

ried Bob Dylan on November 22, 1965. She is a quiet person and a believer in the ancient philosophy of Zen. Many of Dylan's New York friends believe that Sarah added balance to Dylan's often freaky life style.

They have 5 children. The Dylan family lived for a time in Woodstock, New York, and then moved back to the Village. In the early 1970's the Dylans moved to Southern California. There Bob was writing the soundtrack for the film in which he also acted, *Pat Garrett and Billy the Kid.* Shortly after, an album by the same name appeared, heralding a new, loosening-up period for Dylan. This soundtrack was unlike any other in history. It was completely composed and performed by Dylan. Most of the album sounds like Dylan when he is sitting around with a few friends, making nice music.

In *Dylan,* his thirteenth album, Dylan does songs that folk singers such as Joni Mitchell or Joan Baez would sing. The strange thing about the album is that he makes it all sound like a Dylan album.

In *Dylan,* Bob sings a simple la-dee-da-dee-da song titled "Sarah Jane." Again the silent and funny side of Dylan emerges. To the disappointment of curious Dylan fans who hoped to learn something "real" about their hero and his family, Dylan teases: "I've got a wife and five little children. Sarah Jane, Oh! Sarah Jane." Followed by la-dee-da-dee-da and several nonsense verses. Even in song, Dylan pulls the shade on his private life.

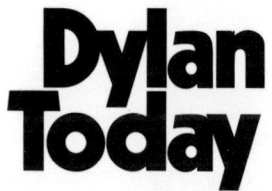

Bob Dylan brought a new truth to popular music: singers don't have to have nice-sounding voices to sing. The music and the message and the way it's put together are enough.

Dylan no longer needs to pretend. He no longer makes up fancy stories about himself and his past. He finds more to life with his family and friends than he did with a never-ending string of concert tours and recording sessions.

But Dylan has not retired. He still appears, still sings, and still needs his public. But he needs them as outsiders and appreciators—not as intruders on his private life.

Bob likes the freedom of his life style now. A very rich man, Dylan has attempted to repay people who once helped him through hard times. He has also returned to his childhood religion of Judaism, making regular trips to Israel and giving concerts to support war-torn Israel.

Bob Dylan came on like a sudden wind. He traded the cold, northerly winds of Minnesota for the ever changing winds of Greenwich Village. In 2 short years he was famous. The winds of that fame carried him for 4 more years.

He wrote songs about people, songs about love, songs of protest. He put big ideas into everyday words. He told people that the times were changing. He wrote about himself and his loneliness, hoping others would look at themselves and their loneliness.

Bob Dylan's music is as old as the mountains and as new as plexiglass. Most of the melodies he uses are borrowed, revised, turned inside out from ages gone past.

The roaring welcome of a half-million fans for the 1974 concert tour proves that Dylan's words—the old ones and the new ones—still carry powerful messages.

Bob Dylan, the magical song maker of the 60's, is alive and singing. Dylan's words will continue to blow in the wind for a long, long time.

JACKSON FIVE
CARLY SIMON
BOB DYLAN
JOHN DENVER
THE BEATLES
ELVIS PRESLEY
JOHNNY CASH
CHARLEY PRIDE
ARETHA FRANKLIN
ROBERTA FLACK
STEVIE WONDER

Rock'n PopStars